PRACTICAL
ECONOMICS
FOR TEENS

A TEEN GUIDE TO
Buying Goods
and
SERVICES

Tammy
Gagne

Mitchell Lane
PUBLISHERS
P.O. Box 196
Hockessin, Delaware 19707

PRACTICAL ECONOMICS FOR TEENS

A Teen Guide to Buying Goods and Services
A Teen Guide to Earning Income
A Teen Guide to Protecting and Insuring Assets
A Teen Guide to Saving and Investing

Copyright © 2014 by Mitchell Lane Publishers

Printing 1 2 3 4 5 6 7 8 9

ABOUT THE AUTHOR: Tammy Gagne has authored dozens of books for both adults and children over the last decade. Several of her titles, including *A Dividend Stock Strategy for Teens* and *A Teen Guide to Safe-Haven Savings* for Mitchell Lane Publishers, focus on finances. Teaching her own teenage son to be a savvy consumer has long been one of her biggest priorities. She thinks all young people should understand how the economy works. By striking a balance between shrewd saving and conscious spending, teens can become the change that is needed in our economy.

Library of Congress Cataloging-in-Publication Data

Gagne, Tammy.
  A teen guide to buying goods and services / by Tammy Gagne.
      pages cm. — (Practical economics for teens)
  Includes bibliographical references and index.
  Audience: Age 9-13.
  Audience: Grade 4 to 8.
  ISBN 978-1-61228-472-9 (library bound)
  1. Teenage consumers—Juvenile literature.
  2. Consumer education—Juvenile literature.
  3. Consumer goods—Juvenile literature.
  4. Service industries—Juvenile literature. I. Title.
  HC79.C6G333 2014
  640.73—dc23
                                                      2013023028
eBook ISBN: 9781612285283

                                                      PLB

CONTENTS

CHAPTER 1

What Are
GOODS AND SERVICES?

You might think of the economy as something that is driven by the adults of this world. After all, it is adults who earn, save, and spend most of the money. Either one or both of your parents, for example, probably works about forty hours each week. They use the money they earn to pay for the things your family needs. As consumers, they pay for the home that you live in, the clothes that you wear, and the food that you eat. But did you know that you are a consumer as well?

When children are young, their parents make all their buying decisions. From diapers and car seats to books and toys, your parents had to choose these items for you. As you got older, though, you began making some choices of your own. Today you probably make many buying decisions without even realizing it. Your room may be part of your parents' home, but you probably picked the posters that hang on your walls. Most likely you also had some say in selecting the clothes in your closet. You might even ask your parents to buy a certain breakfast cereal brand that is your favorite. These products are all examples of goods.

In addition to goods, you may also have a say in many of the services your parents purchase. For example, who cuts your hair? Do you take guitar or piano lessons? Or go to camp over the summer? Services are benefits that are not

You may not even realize it, but the last time you went shopping for new clothes, you played an active role in the economy. Perhaps you also received a manicure or pedicure while you were at the mall. When people spend money on goods and services like these, it helps the economy grow.

Some services, like music lessons, are ongoing. The cost of a single lesson may not seem like much, but weekly lessons can add up. Think of how much money your parents have spent on guitar lessons if you have been playing for an entire year.

physical items and cannot be owned. Together, goods and services make up an important part of our economy.

A long time ago, goods and services were obtained a different way. A person who had a talent for producing a certain type of good or for performing a specific type of service would make a deal with a person who could fulfill a different need. This exchange of goods and services for other goods and services was called trade. Let's say you raised chickens and your neighbor raised sheep. You could get enough wool to knit a sweater for each member of your family by agreeing to provide your neighbor with a certain number of fresh eggs.

But what would happen if your neighbor with the wool already had an agreement with the farmer up the road who also raised chickens? Consumers had to find a way of getting the goods and services they needed in situations like this one. The answer to this problem was money. The sheep farmer could still trade with people who offered the goods and services he needed, but he could also do business with other people. Adding money into the equation helped expand business. Today trade more commonly refers to the exchange of goods and services for money.

When people spend money, their spending contributes to the growth of the economy. By buying goods and services, consumers provide income to the businesses that offer them. These businesses can then use the money they earn to produce more products or expand the services they offer. When companies grow, they need more workers. This need creates jobs for people who want to make money. They in turn put a large amount of this money back into the economy when they spend it as consumers. As long as consumers are spending money, this cycle continues—improving the economy.

But when people worry that jobs and money are becoming scarce, they spend less. They may fear that their personal income will be reduced, and they want to make sure they will have enough left to pay for the things that they really need. Whether the economy is good or bad, saving money is a smart move. At the same time, a drop in consumer spending takes income away from businesses. Without positive cash flow, companies cannot afford to create new jobs. Sometimes they even have to eliminate jobs. Until spending increases, this cycle also continues—in this case, worsening the economy instead of improving it.

Bear in mind that goods and services aren't always about fun and luxury. When consumers aren't spending money on new cars or family vacations, their money is still going somewhere. Let's say that your parents decide to keep their older car instead of buying a new one. What happens to the money that they would have spent on the new vehicle?

One place it is likely going is into their gas tank. One of the reasons that your parents opted not to buy another car just now may be the rising cost of gasoline. From 2009 to 2011, gas prices rose 67 percent—from under $2 per gallon to over $3 per gallon.[1] In some states, gas prices are over $4 a gallon.

This spike in the cost of gasoline has led to price increases for many other products and services as well. Let's consider the cost of that breakfast cereal brand you like best as an example. When the prices of grains and other ingredients rise, the cost of making products like cereal also rises. Companies may not raise their prices right away, though. They don't want to lose customers by charging more than other companies for similar products. Another cost businesses must consider is transportation. When the cost of shipping the cereal across the country goes up due to rising gas prices, the company that makes your cereal may have no choice but to raise its price.

Of course, cereal isn't the only food product that has risen in price. Most products at the grocery store cost more today than they did just a year ago. In fact over the last several years food prices have risen by about 3 percent each year. And they are expected to keep rising.[2] A rise in the general level of prices is called inflation. When this happens, the value of your money decreases—because it can't buy as much as it could before.

Marilyn Geewax is a senior business editor for National Public Radio (NPR). She shared a different way of looking at rising food prices on the NPR program *Talk of the Nation*. Although the prices of most foods are higher than they used to be, a smaller part of a paycheck is needed to buy certain things. "In 1900, to buy a dozen eggs, it took a little bit more than an hour's worth of work for the average person. You were making about 21 cents an hour, and a dozen eggs cost about 23 cents," she explained. "So that was a lot of work to serve your family a dozen eggs. So just to understand how much the prices have actually fallen over time, the typical wage now is about $23 an hour, and eggs are, you know, $1.69, maybe $2 depending on what you're buying. So it takes a fraction of your hour. You can make enough money to buy a dozen eggs in a matter of minutes these days. So it's important for us to remember that."[3]

In addition to food and other basic goods that we buy, we also need certain services even when we are cutting back on our spending. If your parents keep that older car, they won't have a payment, but they may need to spend

Goods and Services Tips and Trivia

In addition to being consumers, many teens also create and sell goods and services. Perhaps you have turned a hobby like jewelry-making into a small business by selling bracelets and earrings on eBay. If so, you're producing and selling goods. Or maybe you have a part-time job at a restaurant. In this case, you are part of the service industry.

money on repairs more often than they did before. Businesses like auto repair shops now end up with some of that money that your parents would have spent on a new car.

Instead of spending several thousand dollars on a tropical vacation, your parents may spend some of their cash on other forms of family entertainment. Maybe they will choose to buy a new LED television or Blu-ray player so the family can enjoy watching movies together at home. Whether they spend a little or a lot, purchasing these goods has an effect on the country's economy.

Your spending also affects the economy, even when money is tight. Perhaps you get your money from your parents, like 42 percent of teens do. Or maybe you earn an allowance or work at a part-time job, like 52 percent of young people do.[4] Either way you are choosing which goods and services fit your needs (and wants) nearly every day. Even when you aren't spending money, chances are good you are thinking about what you will spend it on later. This is the reason that so many television commercials are aimed at young people. Tune in to a channel geared towards teens, and then count the number of ads that you see.

Goods and Services Tips and Trivia

Part of being smart about money is knowing exactly what you are getting for your money. Don't be fooled by a new low price if the size of the package is smaller than it used to be. Many companies try to make it seem like they aren't raising their prices by using this somewhat deceiving technique. Your box of cereal may still cost $3, but if it contains fewer servings than it did before, you are actually paying more for each one of them.

CHAPTER 2

They Want YOU!

Teenagers make up a powerful demographic in the world of advertising. Although the word sounds complicated, a demographic is simply a group of people who have something in common, like age. Companies usually aim to sell their products to specific demographics. Young people make up the biggest demographic in many areas of business.

Part of the reason that companies target teens is that there are so many of them—more than 25 million in the United States alone. Another reason that businesses market their products to teens is that they have money. The money spent on products for teenagers totaled more than $208 billion in 2012. Kids between 12 and 14 years of age earn an average of $2,167 each year. For teens between 15 and 17, this number nearly doubles—to $4,023 per year.[1] Because kids have so few expenses, most of this cash is considered discretionary income, money that they can spend on whatever they choose.

Just as important as the money itself, teens are often easily influenced by advertising. Today an American teenager can see an ad almost anywhere. From television to magazines, and billboards to websites, companies are paying lots of money to make sure you know about their products. Teens are more likely to base their buying decisions on whether a product will help them fit in with other people their age, and

Sales are just one of the ways that retail stores get people to spend money. You might consider buying an item that you didn't even think you needed yesterday if it is being sold at a deep discount today. Just remember that you must be able to afford the cost, even if it is a great deal.

many ads aim to convince teens that their products will do just that. In this way peer pressure drives much of the advertising directed at people in this age group. Think of how many companies hire young, fit celebrities to appear in their ad campaigns. These businesses use the image of a famous person to appeal to young consumers.

Teenagers don't have to be victims when it comes to marketing, though. When you see an advertisement, ask yourself how much actual information about the product it contains. Many ads focus on dazzling graphics or catchy jingles instead of providing real information about the product. These commercials try to sell goods by getting you to associate them with a positive feeling. For example, an ad for an acne cream may show a group of good-looking teenagers riding around in a convertible with upbeat music playing. The actors are all smiling and having a good time, and the company probably hopes that you will link their product to having cool friends and lots of fun.

Even when ads do make statements about the products, listen carefully to the claims. Do they sound reasonable? Does the product come with any type of guarantee? If the item isn't all you had hoped, will you be sorry you spent your money? Beware of companies that make unrealistic promises. When something seems too good to be true, it usually is.

Advertising targeted at teens isn't a new concept, but it is changing along with advancing technology. Not only are teens big buyers of electronic goods, but today they also use that technology to do the buying. Eighty-four percent of teens shop online regularly.[2] Although you usually pay a shipping fee for items purchased this way, you can save a lot more than the shipping amount by using the internet to comparison shop. How long would it take you to visit ten different stores in person to find their prices for a particular

Everything looks better through "COOL" shades!

Take enough time to make sure that you truly want or need an item before you buy it. You might even want to stop and ask yourself if you are falling for an advertising scheme. Sometimes all it takes to see through an ad is looking at it from a slightly different perspective.

item? You might even spend more money on gas than you would pay to ship the item to your home.

By shopping online, teens may be saving money in more ways than one. According to a recent study by the California Institute of Technology, consumers are willing to pay up to 50 percent more for products that they can touch.[3] What does this mean to you? You will probably make much smarter buying decisions when you shop online. Despite this perk, 78 percent of teenage girls still prefer in-store shopping. The number for guys was similar, with 75 percent of male teens opting to visit a store rather than shop online.[4]

Among the least likely places to find teens shopping in person are music stores. Only 13 percent of teens still buy CDs in stores. Fifty-five percent say they download music online through services like iTunes instead. Another 23 percent don't buy music at all. They use internet radio programs like Pandora for listening to music.[5]

Businesses that do make their money from in-store purchases also use technology to attract teens. Nearly every retailer these days offers an app for your smartphone. You might use one of these programs to look through a virtual flyer or read product reviews. You can even use a mobile device to download coupons that you can redeem by simply showing the screen to clerks.

The smartest retailers are taking full advantage of technology by reaching teens through advertising online. At one time the best way to reach teens was through television commercials. Today, though, teens are watching less television. In 2013, teens watched an average of twenty-one hours and twenty-two minutes of television each week, down

Goods and Services Tips and Trivia

Businesses don't just gear advertising toward teens. They also make their goods or services appealing to young people in other ways. Products aimed at a young demographic are often packaged in fun ways. They may even come with free gifts that encourage kids to buy them. Restaurants that cater to teens might have trendy decor with comfortable seating to win more teenage business.

With MY PHONE's 4G smartphones, not only do you get unlimited calling and texting, WiFi internet access, and many other features, you can also photograph yourself with a friend and share your photo with all your friends!

With your purchase, receive a $25 off coupon for any of our featured cell phone cases.

This ad uses several advertising ploys. In addition to featuring attractive young people, it also shows them having a great time with this phone. The company is selling that great time just as much as the phone itself. Finally, it also offers a $25 off coupon good towards a phone case.

12 percent from 2011.[6] Instead of watching television, teens are spending more time on the internet, making the World Wide Web one of the best places for companies to spend their advertising dollars.

Smartphones also serve as a great delivery system for advertisers. Nielsen reports that teens are the fastest growing audience for mobile content. Young people between the ages of 12 and 17 watch nearly twice as much mobile video as other consumers.[7] Whether you are catching up on the news and weather or watching the latest episode of your favorite reality show online, chances are good that an ad will appear along with the content. If you don't have to

Young shoppers are becoming smarter about how they spend their money. By only shopping when they need something and paying attention to prices, they can make their money go further. By shopping the sales, you might be able to buy two items for the price of one—or save the difference.

watch a commercial before the video plays, there are probably at least one or two ads running alongside your video window. Chances are also pretty good that many of these ads are directed at people in your age group.

Even though teens make up a significant part of the consumer population, one thing is for certain: Even young people are interested in saving money these days. An overwhelming majority of teenagers say that the economy has affected their spending habits. About half say they no longer shop for fun, but rather buy things only when they need them. Thirty-three percent only buy items that are on sale.[8]

Retailers are paying attention to these changes. Today teens can find entire stores that cater to thrifty teen shoppers. Tom Vellios is the chief executive officer of Five Below, a retailer that specializes in high-quality, low-cost items that appeal to young people. Every item in the store sells for just $5 or less. As Vellios explained to *The Boston Globe*, "We wanted a place for kids to go after they graduated from the toy store."

From beauty products and clothes to movies and electronics, teens are thinking more before spending. This means that companies must work harder to convince teens to buy their products. One way many companies are attracting young people is through loyalty reward programs. Shoppers who sign up for these programs earn credits for the purchases they make. When they build up enough credits, they receive a gift card or coupon. Many shoppers will spend more money if they are working toward a goal like this one. Other companies charge a small fee for a membership card that offers them better prices on certain merchandise than non-cardholders pay.

Goods and Services Tips and Trivia

One of the best ways that companies advertise their products is word of mouth. Many teens want to buy items that they see their friends using. Think about your favorite brand of sneakers. Now consider how many of your friends own shoes made by this same manufacturer. Do you really like this product, or do you like the idea of having the most popular brand at the moment?

CHAPTER 3
Making Green by
SELLING GREEN

Among the most popular types of goods that both adults and teens buy are so-called green products. Being kind to the environment and making healthier choices have become growing priorities for many people. This desire to take care of the earth and to fill our bodies with food grown without synthetic chemicals or genetic modification has led to a whole new realm of goods and services.

Nearly every grocery store now offers at least some organic products. Some food stores have entire sections devoted to organic goods. You can even find businesses that only sell organic food.

In addition to organic food, many consumers like to buy other products that were made with the welfare of the environment in mind. These green goods include items made at factories that keep pollution to a minimum. There was a time when most people bought items without really thinking about how they were made. In recent decades consumers have realized that many companies produce large amounts of dangerous chemicals as a by-product of manufacturing. These chemicals are released into the surrounding air, water, or both. Pollutants like these hurt the earth, wildlife, and even people who live nearby. For this reason many consumers prefer to do business with companies who use a green approach to manufacturing.

Do you have a reusable water bottle? Whether it is made of plastic, aluminum, or stainless steel, buying this item once is better for the environment than buying bottled water over and over. Plus, you save money each time you refill your own bottle.

Of course, it's not just companies making goods that pollute the environment. Many service-based businesses do their share of harm to the environment as well. For example, more than 60 percent of the world's electricity is produced by power plants that burn fossil fuels.[1] This process releases massive amounts of carbon into the environment. You may have heard the term carbon footprint. This phrase refers to the amount of carbon that a person or company produces over time. Carbon footprints are important, because the element is thought by some people to be the biggest contributor to global warming. Just one power plant that burns fossil fuels can produce millions of tons of carbon each year.

Other green products include those that decompose quickly without hurting the earth and those that can be recycled easily. Biodegradable products are items that break down after they are thrown away. Not all biodegradable products decompose at the same rate, though. Technically, a plastic water bottle will break down over time, but it can take hundreds or thousands of years. Many consumers prefer to buy reusable water bottles made of aluminum or steel for this reason. You can find these eco-friendly bottles in a wide array of bright colors and designs that companies produce just for young people.

Products made with post-consumer recycled material are also popular with young people who want to buy

THINK GREEN

green goods. Plastic bottles can be used to make some surprising items. They can be turned into backpacks, fleece clothing, paint, and even kayaks. Buyers interested in buying goods made from recycled materials should always check the label before making a purchase. It states the percentage of recycled materials that were used in making the item.

Teenagers today are much more aware of the environment, and they are making a greater effort to reduce, reuse, and recycle than previous generations. Many young people check to see if a product or its packaging is recyclable before buying it. They might even choose one product over another based on this information.

Some young people also work to educate others about the importance of green packaging. In 2012, teenager Abby Goldberg created an online petition in her home state of Illinois. In all she collected more than 173,000 signatures to encourage Governor Pat Quinn to veto a bill that would have prevented Illinois communities from charging for the use of plastic bags or banning them. In the end the governor did indeed veto the bill, in large part due to Abby's efforts.

Abby wants her town of Grayslake to ban plastic bags altogether. "Sea turtles swallow plastic bags, thinking they're jellyfish, and sea birds get trapped in them. They get caught

Goods and Services Tips and Trivia

When you consider how green a company is, consider how much money or how many of its goods it donates to eco-friendly charities. Making biodegradable products or items made from recycled materials is important, but how a business shares its wealth can also make a big difference to the environment.

in trees and they just harm our environment," she told the *Daily Herald*.[2]

Sarah Kirch is the director of development at Prairie Crossing Charter School, where Abby learned about this issue in an environmental awareness class. Kirch told the newspaper, "For a (12- or 13-year-old) to accomplish something of this scale, it's really astounding. It shows the power of what youth can accomplish."[3]

Of course, not every young person goes to the lengths that Abby did in trying to get governments and businesses to make eco-friendly changes. Other young people show their power with how they choose to spend their money, and companies who want them as customers are listening. Fast food restaurants like Chipotle Mexican Grill have made it part of their companies' mission to serve healthy food that is grown with respect for the environment.

Chipotle's website proudly states, "Currently, 40 percent of our beans are organically grown, which has a number of benefits including a reduction of more than 140,000 pounds of chemical pesticide since 2005. We have been increasing our use of organically grown beans over the last few years and may use even more in the coming years."[4]

This popular company also shares with its customers that being green is about protecting valuable natural resources. "Organic is great, but it's not always appropriate

One of the easiest ways to have organic food is growing it yourself in your own backyard. When you plant, grow, and prepare your own fruits and vegetables, you know exactly what has been done to the food. Keeping a garden is also much cheaper than buying organic produce at the supermarket.

for the food we serve," Chipotle explains. "Sometimes we can find farmers who focus on responsible or sustainable practices but aren't certified organic. We make that call market-by-market, ingredient-by-ingredient, always keeping the big picture in mind."[5] They must be doing something right, because teens are flocking to Chipotle locations. A restaurant survey by Piper Jaffray ranked the restaurant as the number-two choice of places to eat among teens.[6]

Consumers who buy green products must usually spend a little more than they would on non-green options. Many shoppers are willing to do just that, though, even in a struggling economy. Marshal Cohen is the chief industry analyst for the research firm The NPD Group. As he explained to *Women's Wear Daily*, "While many people may have believed green was gone due to the economic downturn, by no means is that true."[7] Cohen even thinks that green products could help to improve the state of the economy.

Reinier Evers, founder of Trendwatching.com, agrees. He told the trade journal, "Recession or not, consumers will continue to demand responsible behavior."[8] One company that is responding to this demand is Payless ShoeSource, a company known for its inexpensive but trendy footwear. Payless's zoe&zac brand is made for those who want to buy green without spending tons of cash. All the shoes, handbags, and beauty products from the line are made from green materials like hemp or organic cotton. The shoes have recycled rubber outsoles, include eco-friendly cushioning, and are assembled with water-based glues. Even the shoeboxes are green, made with recycled material and soy-based ink. Teens can find a wide variety of styles, all under $35.

Customers who buy from this green product line are also helping the environment in another way. The Plant a Billion Trees campaign plans to rebuild the Atlantic Forest in Brazil by 2015. Payless donates a portion of every sale from the zoe&zac line to this environmental cause. Consumers get the green products they want at a price they can afford, and they can feel good knowing that some of the money is going to a green charity.

Consumers are buying this feeling as much as the products themselves. Bill D'Arienzo is the founder and chief executive officer of WDA BrandMarketing Solutions. He thinks that giving consumers more control is the secret to improving the economy. "In these tough times, consumers want to feel good by knowing they are doing good," he explained. "Buying sustainable products lets them feel they have control over their environment and economy, which both seem to them to be out of control."[9]

Goods and Services Tips and Trivia

If you believe in recycling, consider buying used items instead of new goods whenever possible. Buying pre-owned items helps to reduce waste, and it will also save you money. To continue the cycle, be sure to pass your unwanted items on to other people who can use them. You can sell or auction them off online or donate them to your favorite charity.

Made in the
USA

Some people think the biggest reason that the United States economy is in such poor shape is that we import too many goods from other countries. Take a quick look around your home, and it may take you a while to find an item labeled "Made in the USA." It might be almost as difficult to find an item that wasn't made in China. A large number of the manufactured goods sold in the United States come from this foreign country.

Items made in China generally cost less than similar items made in the United States or elsewhere. The reason for this difference is that Chinese companies pay their workers considerably less than American companies do. The cost of labor is a big factor in the price of many items; therefore, consumers save money by buying goods imported from this country. They may be paying a higher price in other ways, though.

Roger Simmermaker is the author of How Americans Can Buy American. The book lists more than twenty thousand products and services that are made in the USA. He explained to Gannett News Service, "It's important to understand that workers in China don't pay taxes to America. Only American workers do. And American companies typically pay twice as much in taxes to the US Treasury compared with foreign-owned companies."[1]

An overwhelming number of electronic items come from countries other than the United States. To find out just how many, start searching through your own electronics. You will likely have a hard time finding even one that was made in the USA.

In addition to paying low wages, China also has a rampant problem with abusive child labor practices. The legal age for working in China is sixteen, but many kids much younger than this are forced to work in harsh conditions for long hours and minimal amounts of pay.

Hu Xingdou is a professor of economics and social policy at the Beijing Institute of Technology. He told *The New York Times* that child labor abuse is typical in the country. "China's economy is developing at a fascinating speed, but often at the expense of laws, human rights, and environmental protection." China is also known for its loose pollution regulations for factories. "Most of the work force comes from underdeveloped or poverty-stricken areas," the professor said. "Some children are even sold by their parents, who often don't have any idea of the working conditions."[2]

Even people who aren't concerned about the US economy find these practices deplorable. When American consumers learn about these horrendous human rights violations, many decide to take a stand against buying Chinese goods. After all, these companies cannot sell their

merchandise without buyers. This is when most consumers realize the magnitude of the problem. For most people in the United States, boycotting all Chinese-made goods simply isn't possible. But you can make an effort to increase the number of American-made items you buy.

According to ABC News, the average American spends $700 on holiday shopping each year. If each person spent just $64 of this amount on goods made in the United States, the effort would create two hundred thousand new jobs for Americans.[3] Remember, the money that consumers spend helps existing companies to expand their workforces. A higher demand for American-made products could also be an incentive for new companies to go into business here.

Consumers shouldn't assume that dealing with an American business means buying American-made items. It isn't just Chinese companies that are making goods in China. American businesses too are manufacturing goods in this overseas location and selling them here at home. Numerous US companies, some of them extremely large, have chosen to move their factories to China, Mexico, and other foreign countries where they can pay less to make their products. Many American companies also pay Chinese workers to make certain parts of their products.

Adam and Julie Reiser founded a business that helps consumers be certain that they are buying American-made merchandise. Their service-based business, which they call Made in the USA Certified, confirms that a company's claims of producing goods made in the USA are accurate. "Buying something that is made in the USA is something to be proud of," Julie told Gannett News Service. "It always makes the consumer feel good, that they're helping out the economy by keeping the money at home and helping protect jobs here."[4]

Not everyone thinks that buying from China is a bad thing. The Chinese government insists that it is working to stop labor violations within the country. The country does have labor laws in place that set a minimum age for workers and limitations on the number of hours that employers can utilize them. Companies that force minors to work are violating these laws.

Many Americans see trading with China as a valuable part of the US economy, not its downfall. Baizhu Chen is a professor at the University of Southern California's Marshall School of Business. In an article he wrote for *Forbes* magazine, Professor Chen explained that many products that are made in China are sold by American retailers. These companies pay taxes and employ American workers. "Minnesota-based Target, with more than 1,200 stores nationwide selling lots of China-made merchandise," he pointed out, "employs over 350,000 American workers."[5]

Laura Baughman is the president of the Trade Partnership, a firm in Washington, DC, that consults with businesses on matters of trade. This company asserts that imports from China actually help to create about 1 million jobs here in the United States. Baughman explained to *USA Today*, "Because we import from China, prices are cheaper, consumers have more money in their pocket, and they go out and spend more."[6]

A recent study by the Federal Reserve Bank of San Francisco revealed that 55 percent of the money spent on goods imported from China actually goes to US businesses. American marketing and sales is largely responsible for creating this revenue. The study also found that only 2.7 percent of US consumer spending goes to China each year. Bart Hobijn is a senior researcher who worked on the study. He pointed out to *USA Today* that even though products

Goods and Services Tips and Trivia

If you want to find out exactly how much money you spend on goods made in foreign countries, try an experiment. For the next month, buy only items that were made entirely in the United States. Doing so will help you identify the goods that are the most difficult to find with a "Made in the USA" label. You may also discover some great new brands that are manufactured right here at home.

imported from China are numerous, consumer spending is about a lot more than buying goods. "If you get a haircut, pay your electricity bill, go to the movies, that's all part of consumption."[7]

An overwhelming majority of goods sold in the United States are also made here. Clothing and shoes are among the biggest exceptions, mostly because of cost. American companies find it hard to compete with China's prices on these items. American-made products are out there, though. For some young people these buying decisions are based on style and price rather than where an item was manufactured. However consumers go about making up their minds, almost 36 percent of the money Americans spend on clothing goes to garments made in China. American-made items fetch 25 percent of clothing cash.[8]

China also isn't the only foreign country whose goods Americans buy. You probably purchase items made all over the globe, whether you realize it or not. The United States imports products from companies in other countries in Asia, as well as from businesses in Australia, Europe, Africa, and North and South America.

Just as importantly, the United States also exports items to other countries, including China. According to the US-China Business Council, the number of items that the United States sold to China increased by 468 percent between 2000 and 2010. We sold a total of $91.9 billion worth of goods to Chinese consumers in 2010. In this same year, though, the United States imported $364.9 billion worth of Chinese goods—nearly four times the value of goods we sold.[9]

Many Americans think that we should limit our spending on Chinese-made items until this trade deficit is lowered. Some think that we should buy American whenever possible regardless of how many items Chinese consumers are buying from us. But no matter how you choose to buy, the most important thing you can do is to become a well-informed consumer yourself. Before you buy any product, do a little research to find out where it is made. If you are comfortable buying items imported from other countries, you may indeed be helping the United States by doing so. At the very least, though, you should know where your money is going.

Goods and Services Tips and Trivia

Among the most popular goods that the United States imports from China are electronics and machines, toys and games, furniture and clothing, and footwear. The most popular goods we import from Mexico include electronics, vehicles (including parts for cars and trucks), mineral fuel and oil, and precious metals such as gold and silver.

One of the most expensive items people buy is furniture. If you are looking for a new dresser or other large piece of furniture, consider buying it from a company that manufactures its products in the USA. By doing so you will be keeping hundreds of dollars in the economy right here at home.

CHAPTER 5

Consumer Rights and
RESPONSIBILITIES

Being a consumer comes with a lot of responsibility. Finding reasonably priced products that are made without hurting either people or the environment can be a challenge, but it is well worth the effort. Many people see responsible spending as an investment of sorts. When you buy green goods, you are helping green businesses grow. When you buy American-made products, you are helping your country's economy prosper. As an American consumer, you also have rights.

Until the 1950s consumers had very few rights. People who spent money on goods and services basically took the risk of not getting what they should when shelling out their cash. This all began to change on March 15, 1962. This was the day that President John F. Kennedy established the Consumer Bill of Rights. The list was adopted by the United Nations General Assembly in 1985 to create similar standards for the sale of goods and services worldwide. Today March 15 is known as World Consumer Rights Day.

The Consumer Bill of Rights originally consisted of four rights; today there are eight basic rights that every customer in the United States can expect from businesses that offer goods or services. The first of these is the right to choose. Neither the government nor any private company can force you to buy a specific product or service. As a consumer in this country, you may deal with the business of your choice.

Listening to digital music on a computer and/or on MP3 players has become enormously popular in recent years. Consumers don't even have to leave the comfort of their homes to buy their favorite songs. And unlike other types of online shopping, buying digital music offers instant gratification. No shipping required—just click and listen.

Goods and Services Tips and Trivia

Some companies make money by scamming inexperienced consumers. If you receive an email about a particular product or service, be sure to check the company out before buying. Avoid clicking on links that appear in these emails, as they can lead you to imposter companies and even computer viruses. Instead, search for the company independently, and do thorough research before making a purchase.

This consumer right also makes competition among sellers possible. When companies have to compete against one another for your business, they must strive to offer the best products and services at the best possible prices. Since you can spend your money anywhere, these companies need to give you a reason to choose to do business with them.

The second right on the list is the right to safety. When an American consumer purchases a product or service, it shouldn't cause harm in any way when used properly. The third right states that consumers are entitled to information about the products they purchase. This information can help them make the best possible decisions with their money. Let's say that you are allergic to wool. Perhaps wearing any garment made from this material causes you to break out in a horrible rash. For you wool is harmful. But it isn't the second right that applies to you, since most people can indeed wear clothes made from this fiber. The third rule, however, makes it possible for you to check a sweater's label before you buy it. Doing so helps you avoid the situation altogether.

The fourth right on the Consumer Bill of Rights is the right to be heard. This means that the people of the United States can share their opinions when new policies about consumerism are created. It also means that you have the right to have your complaint heard if you think that you have been treated unfairly as a consumer. In this case, if the business itself does not address your concerns, the government will. Americans can contact their state's attorney general for help.

The fifth right, the right to redress, takes the fourth right a bit further. Let's say that you buy an MP3 player, but when you get it home, it doesn't work. In this situation most stores will allow you to exchange the faulty merchandise for a player that does function properly. Some may even offer to refund your money when you return the faulty item. If not, though, you have the right to sue the company for selling you something that was broken.

The sixth right on the list states that consumers are entitled to environmental health. This means that they can expect not to suffer from any ill effects from air, land, or water pollution that is caused by a company's operations. If a business is dumping waste material in a river, for example, the Consumer Bill of Rights affords the people who live near the waterway the right to hold the company responsible for its actions. Ultimately, the company would have to discontinue this dangerous practice and likely pay damages to anyone who has been negatively affected.

The seventh right entitles consumers to the right to satisfaction of basic needs. This right says that consumers

If you buy an item that doesn't work, return it to the store promptly and ask to exchange it. If the salesperson refuses to give you a new item in exchange for the defective one, tell him or her that you are entitled to a replacement under the Consumer Bill of Rights.

should have access to goods and services that are basic and essential. Things like food, clothing, shelter, and water are included in this right.

Finally, everyone in the United States has the right to consumer education. Whether we are new to buying goods and services, or we simply want to know about any new policies that have been enacted by the government, each one of us is entitled to learn about our rights and responsibilities as consumers. In addition to the information you can find at government websites, you can also find businesses whose mission is to educate consumers as thoroughly as possible.

Before you make a large purchase of any kind, it is smart to begin by checking the company's rating with the Better Business Bureau (BBB). This private, nonprofit organization has been around even longer than the Consumer Bill of Rights. The BBB was founded in 1912 and has local chapters all over the country. At BBB.org, consumers can find ratings (from A+ to F) and other information about particular companies. You can even file a formal complaint against a company if you would like the BBB to help you resolve a problem you have had.

Critics of the BBB say that the organization cannot be impartial because it collects fees from member companies. A 2010 ABC News report revealed that Southern California businesses were told they had to pay if they wanted an "A" rating. Carrie Hurt, the president and CEO of the BBB says that they have since expelled the company that ran the Southern California chapter. "Our ratings are not for sale," she said.[1]

Goods and Services Tips and Trivia

You can find back issues of *Consumer Reports* magazine at many libraries across the country. You can also purchase a subscription to the *Consumer Reports* website, which will give you access to reviews of numerous types of products, not just those featured in the current issue of the magazine.

Another way to find information about products and services is by reading *Consumer Reports*. This monthly magazine publishes reviews and other information about a wide range of popular goods and services. The publication has an excellent reputation among consumers, largely because it does not make its money from advertising like other magazines. Certainly, other publications can write accurate articles about products that may interest readers, but if they give a product a negative review, these magazines risk losing that company's advertising dollars. Since *Consumer Reports* doesn't depend on advertising to make money, it is considered one of the most impartial sources for consumer information.

Companies that offer goods or services must live up to consumer expectations if they want to thrive. Consumers too have responsibilities, however. The first is to use the products they buy for their intended purposes. If you fall while using a chair as a stepstool, any injury that you suffer is not the responsibility of the company that built this piece of furniture. If, however, you fall while sitting in the chair because the leg is faulty, that is another story—one that you should tell the company when you return the merchandise, or the Better Business Bureau if the company refuses to address the problem.

Also, you have a responsibility to follow any instructions that come with the products you buy. Let's say that a garment's label explicitly tells you to wash the item by hand and let it line dry. If you toss it into the washing machine or dryer and it discolors or shrinks, you cannot expect the company to replace the item or refund your money.

If you do have a poor experience, you also have a responsibility to share it with other consumers. If a product doesn't work as well as it promised or if a business provides a low level of service, write a review. Many online companies now offer their customers the opportunity to rate the products they buy. Be honest, fair, and as thorough as possible in your assessments. Doing so will help other people make informed decisions when they consider the same items.

You should also read reviews that others have posted online, but be cautious. Some businesses pay other companies to continually write positive reviews for their products and services. They may also post unfair negative reviews about other companies. To combat this practice, Amazon.com lets you know which reviews were written by people who actually purchased the product through their site. Look for the words "Amazon Verified Purchase" before these reviews. Similarly, Yelp.com allows reviewers to check in to local businesses using their smartphones to prove that they actually visited the location. Although these safeguards can't stop all fraudulent reviews, they can give you a better chance of finding real reviews. And those reviews just might save you the trouble of a bad experience in the first place.

Being a smart consumer is about a lot more than buying goods and services. It is also about taking the time to make the best decisions possible. Young people have as much to contribute as consumers as adults do. In fact, in the years to come, you will have the most influence on where the world of goods and services is headed. Just imagine the products that your kids will be buying one day, when you are the one handing out the allowance money instead of receiving it.

Chapter 1. What Are Goods and Services?

1. Mark Hemingway, *The Weekly Standard*, "Hope and Change: Gas Prices Have Gone Up 67 Percent Since Obama Became President," March 9, 2011.

2. USDA Economic Research Service, "Change in Food Price Indexes, 2011 through 2014."

3. Neal Conan, *Talk of the Nation,* NPR, "The Ripple Effect From Rising Food Prices," July 25, 2012.

4. *Gale Business Insights: Essentials*, "Teen Spending Habits, Likes and Dislikes," July 15, 2010.

Chapter 2. They Want You!

1. Statistic Brain, "Teenage Consumer Spending Statistics," September 8, 2012.

2. *Gale Business Insights: Essentials*, "Teen Spending Habits, Likes and Dislikes," July 15, 2010.

3. Kristin Samuelson, *Chicago Tribune*, "Let Your Fingers Do the Shopping," October 22, 2010.

4. Marketing Charts, "Teens Vastly Prefer Shopping In-Store to Online; Top Spending Categories Listed," April 11, 2013.

5. Gillian Reagan, *Business Insider,* "What Teens Want: A Fascinating Music and Recession Study," April 27, 2010.

6. Marketing Charts, "Teens Vastly Prefer Shopping In-Store to Online; Top Spending Categories Listed," April 11, 2013

7. Neilsen, "Kids Today How the Class of 2011 Engages With Media," June 8, 2011.

8. *Gale Business Insights: Essentials*, "Teen Spending Habits, Likes and Dislikes," July 15, 2010.

Chapter 3. Making Green by Selling Green

1. US Department of Energy, "International Energy Statistics: Electricity Generation."

2. Steve Zalusky, *Daily Herald*, "Teen Activist Celebrates Plastic Bag Veto," August 27, 2012.

3. Ibid.

4. Chipotle Mexican Grill, "Food With Integrity: Environment."

5. Ibid.

6. Nancy Luna, *Orange County Register*, "Chipotle & Olive Garden Are Top Teen Dining Choices, Survey Says," November 5, 2009.

7. Dick Silverman and Samantha Conti, *Women's Wear Daily*, "Going Green Presents Challenges and Opportunities," July 22, 2009, Volume 198, Issue 15, page 8.

8. Ibid.

9. Ibid.

Chapter 4. Made in the USA

1. Gannett News Service, "In Sluggish Economy, Buying American-Made Products Gets New Emphasis," September 2, 2011.

2. David Barboza, "China Says Abusive Child Labor Ring Is Exposed," *The New York Times*, May 1, 2008.

3. ABC News, "Made in America Christmas: Are You In?"

4. Gannett News Service, "In Sluggish Economy, Buying American-Made Products Gets New Emphasis," September 2, 2011.

5. Baizhu Chen, *Forbes*, "Buying from China Is in Fact Buying American," December 22, 2011.

6. Kathy Chu, *USA Today*, "Buy 'Made in China' Goods? Benefits to US May Surprise You," August 24, 2011.

7. Ibid.

8. Ibid.

9. Ibid.

Chapter 5. Consumer Rights and Responsibilites

1. Cindy Galli, ABC News, "Better Business Bureau Gives Itself an 'F' in Los Angeles," March 12, 2013.

Books

Lawrence, Lane and Tom Ridgeway. *Buying Goods and Services.* New York: Rosen Central, 2012.

Simmermaker, Roger. *How Americans Can Buy American.* Orlando, FL: Consumer Patriotism Corporation, 2008.

Sivertsen, Linda and Tosh Sivertsen. *Generation Green: The Ultimate Teen Guide to Living an Eco-Friendly Life.* New York: Simon Pulse, 2008.

Works Consulted

ABC News. "Made in America Christmas: Are You In?" http://abcnews.go.com/WN/mailform?id=14998335

Barboza, David. "China Says Abusive Child Labor Ring Is Exposed." *The New York Times,* May 1, 2008. http://www.nytimes.com/2008/05/01/world/asia/01china.html?pagewanted=all&_r=0

Chen, Baizhu. "Buying from China Is in Fact Buying American." *Forbes,* December 22, 2011. http://www.forbes.com/sites/forbesleadershipforum/2011/12/22/buying-from-china-is-in-fact-buying-american/

Chipotle Mexican Grill. "Food With Integrity: Environment." http://www.chipotle.com/en-us/fwi/environment/environment.aspx

Chu, Kathy. "Buy 'Made in China' Goods? Benefits to US May Surprise You." *USA Today,* August 24, 2011. http://usatoday30.usatoday.com/money/world/story/2011-08-24/Buy-Made-in-China-goods-Benefits-to-US-may-surprise-you/50127452/1

Conan, Neal. "The Ripple Effect From Rising Food Prices." *Talk of the Nation,* NPR, July 25, 2012. http://www.npr.org/2012/07/25/157371037/the-ripple-effect-from-rising-food-prices

Gale Business Insights: Essentials. "Teen Spending Habits, Likes and Dislikes." July 15, 2010. http://bi.galegroup.com/essentials/article/GALE|A233061732

Galli, Cindy. "Better Business Bureau Gives Itself an 'F' in Los Angeles." ABC News, March 12, 2013. http://abcnews.go.com/Blotter/business-bureau-los-angeles/story?id=18706507

Gannett News Service. "In Sluggish Economy, Buying American-Made Products Gets New Emphasis." September 2, 2011.

Hemingway, Mark. "Hope and Change: Gas Prices Have Gone Up 67 Percent Since Obama Became President." *The Weekly Standard,* March 9, 2011. http://www.weeklystandard.com/blogs/hope-and-change-gas-prices-have-gone-67-percent-obama-became-president_553930.html

Luna, Nancy. "Chipotle & Olive Garden Are Top Teen Dining Choices, Survey Says." *Orange County Register,* November 5, 2009. http://fastfood.ocregister.com/2009/11/05/starbucks-chipotle-are-favorite-teen-hangouts-survey-says/40547/

Marketing Charts. "Teens Vastly Prefer Shopping In-Store to Online; Top Spending Categories Listed." April 11, 2013. http://www.marketingcharts.com/wp/topics/e-commerce/teens-vastly-prefer-shopping-in-store-to-online-top-spending-categories-listed-28543/

Marketing Charts. "Traditional TV Viewing, by Age." June 12, 2013. http://www.marketingcharts.com/wp/television/are-young-people-watching-less-tv-24817/attachment/nielsen-tv-weekly-viewing-by-age-q1-2011-q1-2013-june2013/

McMahon, Alexa. "Chain Finds a Way to Fulfill the Fickle." *The Boston Globe*, September 9, 2010.

Nielsen. "Kids Today How the Class of 2011 Engages With Media." June 8, 2011. http://www.nielsen.com/us/en/newswire/2011/kids-today-how-the-class-of-2011-engages-with-media.html?utm_source=feedburner&utm_medium=feed&utm_campaign=Feed%253A+NielsenWire+%2528Nielsen+Wire%2529

Reagan, Gillian. "What Teens Want: A Fascinating Music and Recession Study." *Business Insider*, April 27, 2010. http://www.businessinsider.com/what-teens-want-a-music-and-recession-study-2010-4#34-of-teens-download-a-new-song-from-itunes-first-7

Samuelson, Kristin. "Let Your Fingers Do the Shopping." *Chicago Tribune*, October 22, 2010. http://articles.chicagotribune.com/2010-10-22/business/ct-biz-1022-touch-consumers-20101022_1_online-research-products-google

SF Environment (A Department of the City and County of San Francisco). "Targeting Teens." http://www.sfenvironmentkids.org/teacher/lesson_plans/TargetingTeens_6-12_COMBINED.pdf

Silverman, Dick and Samantha Conti. "Going Green Presents Challenges and Opportunities." *Women's Wear Daily*, July 22, 2009, Volume 198, Issue 15, page 8.

Statistic Brain. "Teenage Consumer Spending Statistics." September 8, 2012. http://www.statisticbrain.com/teenage-consumer-spending-statistics/

USDA Economic Research Service. "Change in Food Price Indexes, 2011 through 2014." http://www.ers.usda.gov/data-products/food-price-outlook/data-files/food-price-outlook/cpi.aspx

US Department of Energy. "International Energy Statistics: Electricity Generation." http://www.eia.gov/cfapps/ipdbproject/IEDIndex3.cfm?tid=2&pid=2&aid=12

Zalusky, Steve. "Teen Activist Celebrates Plastic Bag Veto." *Daily Herald*, August 27, 2012.

On the Internet

Alliance for Consumer Education
    http://www.consumered.org/
Better Business Bureau
    http://www.bbb.org/us/
Consumer Reports
    http://www.consumerreports.org/
Green Living
    http://www.greenlivingonline.com/
LifeSmarts: The Ultimate Consumer Challenge
    http://www.lifesmarts.org/
OnGuardOnline.gov: "Avoiding Online Scams"
    http://www.onguardonline.gov/articles/0001-avoiding-online-scams
The University of Arizona: "Consumer Jungle"
    http://www.consumerjungle.org/

biodegradable (bahy-oh-di-GREY-duh-buhl)—Capable of being broken down by living organisms.

boycott (BOI-kot)—To abstain from buying or using.

by-product (BAHY-prod-uhkt)—A secondary product (either useful or waste) that results from the manufacturing of a primary product.

cash flow (KASH FLOH)—The total amount of money being transferred into and out of a business.

consumer (kuhn-SOO-mer)—A person who uses goods or services.

damages (DAM-ij-ez)—The monetary value paid as reimbursement for harm or injury caused.

demographic (dem-uh-GRAF-ik)—A group of people who have something in common.

discretionary income (dih-SKRESH-uh-ner-ee IN-kuhm)—Income that remains after taxes and bills are paid and can be spent or saved as one wishes.

genetic modification (juh-NET-ik mod-uh-fi-KEY-shuhn)—The process of changing the genetic code of an organism, usually to achieve a specific characteristic.

goods—Physical products that satisfy people's wants and needs.

income (IN-kuhm)—Money that comes in.

inflation (in-FLEY-shuhn)—The increasing of the general level of prices over time.

post-consumer (pohst-kuhn-SOO-mer)—Pertaining to material that has already been used and recycled.

redress (ree-DRES)—Making right that which is wrong.

services (SUR-vis-iz): benefits that are not physical items and cannot be owned.

sustainable (suh-STEY-nuh-buhl)—Able to continue long term without depleting natural resources or causing harm to the environment.

synthetic (sin-THET-ik)—Pertaining to compounds created by humans through a chemical process.

trade deficit (TREYD DEF-uh-sit)—The amount by which the cost of a country's imports exceeds the value of its exports.